How Many Light Bulbs Does It Take to Change the World?

HOW MANY LIGHT BULBS DOES IT TAKE TO CHANGE THE WORLD?

MATT RIDLEY

With a commentary by

STEPHEN DAVIES

Institute of
Economic Affairs

First published in Great Britain in 2019 by
The Institute of Economic Affairs
2 Lord North Street
Westminster
London SW1P 3LB
in association with London Publishing Partnership Ltd
www.londonpublishingpartnership.co.uk

The mission of the Institute of Economic Affairs is to improve understanding of the fundamental institutions of a free society by analysing and expounding the role of markets in solving economic and social problems.

A CIP catalogue record for this book is available from the British Library.

ISBN 978-0-255-36785-1

Many IEA publications are translated into languages other than English or are reprinted. Permission to translate or to reprint should be sought from the Director General at the address above.

Typeset in Kepler by T&T Productions Ltd
www.tandtproductions.com

Printed and bound by CPI Group (UK) Ltd, Croydon, CR0 4YY

CONTENTS

Stephen Davies

Steve Davies is Head of Education at the Institute of Economic Affairs in London. From 1979 until 2009 he was Senior Lecturer in the Department of History and Economic History at Manchester Metropolitan University. He has also been a Visiting Scholar at the Social Philosophy and Policy Center at Bowling Green State University in Bowling Green, Ohio, and a programme officer at the Institute for Humane Studies in Arlington, Virginia. A historian, he graduated from St Andrews University in Scotland in 1976 and gained his PhD from the same institution in 1984. He was co-editor with Nigel Ashford of *The Dictionary of Conservative and Libertarian Thought* (Routledge 1991) and wrote several entries for *The Encyclopedia of Libertarianism* edited by Ronald Hamowy (Sage 2008), including the general introduction. He is also the author of *Empiricism and History* (Palgrave Macmillan 2003), *The Wealth Explosion: The Nature and Origins of Modernity* (Edward Everett Root 2019) and of several articles and essays on topics including the private provision of public goods and the history of crime and criminal justice.

Matt Ridley

Matt Ridley's books have sold over a million copies, been translated into 31 languages and won several awards. They include *The Red Queen*, *Genome*, *The Rational Optimist* and *The Evolution of Everything*. Matt joined the House of Lords in February 2013 and has served on the science and technology select committee and the artificial intelligence committee. He was founding chairman of the International Centre for Life in Newcastle. He also created the Mind and Matter column in the *Wall Street Journal* in 2010, and was a columnist for *The Times* from 2013 to 2018. Matt won the Free Enterprise Award from the Institute of Economic Affairs in 2014. He is a fellow of the Royal Society of Literature and of the Academy of Medical Sciences, and a foreign honorary member of the American Academy of Arts and Sciences.

FOREWORD

Almost every schoolchild learns that Thomas Edison invented the light bulb, but did he? And if he had not invented it, would we be still living in the dark?

In the 2018 Hayek Memorial Lecture, on which this book is based, Matt Ridley explains that, in fact, more than twenty other people can lay claim to have invented the light bulb, more or less independently, around the same time. For example, in February 1879 Joseph Swan lit up a lecture room of 700 people using an evacuated glass bulb with a carbon filament through which a current passed. Thomas Edison filed his patent more than eight months later in November 1879. Around the same time, inventors from the UK, Belgium, Russia, Germany, France, Canada and the US also produced or patented glass light bulbs.

This is the common phenomenon known as simultaneous invention. So, while many of us think of the heroic inventor, Ridley argues that the opposite is often true in that the light bulb emerged from the combined technologies and accumulated knowledge of the day, so was bound to emerge sooner or later.

He contends that innovation, by which he means invention, through to development and commercialisation, is the most important unsolved problem in all of human society. We rely on it, but we do not fully understand it, we cannot predict it and we cannot direct it.

He links this to Hayek's arguments that the knowledge required to make society function is dispersed among ordinary people, rather than available centrally and in concentrated form to experts.

In paraphrasing Edison that innovation is mostly about perspiration, not inspiration, Ridley posits the idea that as with all evolutionary systems, you cannot easily hurry innovation. In other words, we cannot invent things before they are ready to be invented.

He goes on to cover the myth that automation destroys more jobs than it creates and discusses how innovation leads to economic growth. He also takes to task recent examples of barriers to innovation, including the German vacuum cleaner industry, large pharmaceutical companies, the UK's National Health Service and the EU's adoption of the precautionary principle. Addressing the issue of intellectual property rights, which often divides classical liberals, he believes that patents and copyrights, originally intended to encourage innovation, have become far more often ways of defending monopolies against disruption, thanks to lobbying from big businesses.

He concludes that innovation is a mysterious and underappreciated process that we discuss too rarely, hamper too much and value too little.

In response, the IEA's Dr Stephen Davies agrees with many of the points made by Ridley, but with a few caveats. He points out that Ridley's argument that innovation is the product not of heroic visionaries or outstanding and rare individuals, but of large numbers of ordinary, enquiring and enterprising people contradicts the ideas of Ayn Rand. In *The Fountainhead*, Rand's thesis is that progress and innovation come from Promethean individuals, with the rest of humanity eventually following them and benefiting from their creativity. Ridley's argument is that innovation is a social phenomenon, with any particular innovation having many parents and originators, most of them forgotten or even unknown. What matters is the social framework of trade and the free exchange of both goods and ideas among people.

Davies also takes issue with Ridley's view that particular innovations cannot happen until the time is ripe. He gives several examples from history of innovative periods and civilisations which suddenly came to an end, arguing that we cannot believe that the breakthrough into sustained innovation that has occurred since the eighteenth century was somehow inevitable, or the conclusion to a long process of cumulative discovery. Instead, he argues that the forces and factors that had brought earlier episodes to an end were unable to do so again. Such forces include both natural reasons such as low population and low population density, but also man-made rules such as restrictions on trade or access to land, which had been originally intended to protect people against unexpected change and to make life more predictable and stable.

The unintended consequence of these limiting factors was that they also hindered and prevented the kind of sustained innovation that would have allowed them to escape from a Malthusian world of scarcity.

Ridley concludes that since innovation is a bottom-up evolutionary process deriving from dispersed knowledge, instead of messing around trying to find a magic way to create innovation, government should focus on removing things that stop it. We should also be aware of Davies's warning that historically innovation has also led to well-meaning responses and actions that limited or prevented change and innovation, and might seek to do so again.

SYED KAMALL

Academic and Research Director at the Institute of Economic Affairs, and Professor of International Relations and Politics at St Mary's University, Twickenham

October 2019

The views expressed in this monograph are, as in all IEA publications, those of the authors and not those of the Institute (which has no corporate view), its managing trustees, Academic Advisory Council members or senior staff.

ACKNOWLEDGEMENTS

The Institute of Economic Affairs thanks CQS for its very generous sponsorship of the 2018 Hayek Memorial Lecture and of this publication.

SUMMARY

- Innovation is a very important source of economic growth. It increases productivity and creates wealth by freeing up resources to be used for other activity and hence more output. Despite its economic importance, innovation is still not fully understood and is difficult to predict.
- In pre-modern societies, institutions and practices worked against innovation. Their main aim was to make life more predictable and stable and to minimise the effects of change, but they hindered or outright prevented the kind of sustained innovation that leads to escape from the Malthusian cage.
- Innovation is the natural and inevitable result of trade and exchange. When people meet, they not only trade material goods but also exchange ideas and knowledge, which can then be combined in new and unexpected ways. The meeting of minds is not just a figure of speech, but an expression of how new ideas arise and are tested collectively.
- Technological innovation is a bottom-up phenomenon that emerges by trial and error among the ideas of ordinary people, not a *deus ex machina* that descends upon a few brilliant minds. It relies on dispersed knowledge which is not available to central planners.

- Picking winners is a mistake. Government attempts to champion new technologies have a long record of failure. Instead of trying to find a magic way to create innovation, governments should focus on removing things that stop it.
- Big companies and state bureaucracies often attempt to stifle innovation in order to prevent competition and maintain their privileged positions. Intellectual property, occupational licensing and government favouritism are ways of keeping innovators out.
- Patents and copyrights have become ways of defending monopolies against disruption, hampering innovation that takes place through the copying and improvement of existing technology. They have created a class of rentiers who gain wealth and income not by innovation but through the monopoly they have been granted by the state. Intellectual property increasingly undermines real property rights in actual physical commodities by limiting the use their owners can make of them in all kinds of intrusive ways.
- While it is sensible to be concerned about the unintended consequences of innovation, the 'precautionary principle' is used by activists to prevent new technologies getting started, even when these are demonstrably safer and better than existing technologies. Both action and inaction create some risk. Standing in the way of an innovation that might do good can cause real harm.
- EU regulation has hampered innovation by introducing excessive precaution, legal uncertainty,

inconsistency with other regulations, technology-prescriptive rules, burdensome packaging requirements and high compliance costs. Post-Brexit, the UK government could decide to adopt the 'innovation principle' to balance the precautionary principle. In essence, this means re-thinking policies if evidence is found that they are going to impede innovation.

- The harmonisation of regulation through 'trade deals' and by transnational regimes such as the EU threatens to undermine innovation by stifling policy competition. The incentives for ruling elites to check innovation are extremely powerful if they no longer need to fear competition in the way that rulers of smaller states do. The current trend to create a global regulatory order threatens to stop innovation in its tracks.

1 HOW MANY LIGHT BULBS DOES IT TAKE TO CHANGE THE WORLD?

Matt Ridley

Let me begin with a paradox. It concerns the light bulb, that clichéd metaphor for innovation, which was itself an innovation in the 1870s.

The paradox is this. Nobody saw the light bulb coming. Nobody predicted its invention. Yet the closer you look at the story of the light bulb, the more inevitable it seems that it was invented when it was.

Robert Friedel has concluded that there are 21 different people who can lay claim to having invented the light bulb more or less independently in the years leading up to its debut. Given that two of them had crucial assistants who did half the work, I call it 23.

There's Thomas Edison, of course, who filed his patent in November 1879. But there's also Joseph Swan, who demonstrated to an audience of 700 people at the Literary and Philosophical Society in Newcastle on 3 February 1879 that he could illuminate a room – for his lecture – with an evacuated glass bulb containing a carbon filament, through which a current passed.

Then there is William Grove, Fredrick de Moleyns and Warren de la Rue also in Britain, and Marcellin Jobard in Belgium, and Alexander Lodygin in Russia, and Heinrich Gobel in Germany, and Jean Eugene Robert-Houdin in France, and Henry Woodward and Matthew Evans in Canada, and Hiram Maxim and John Starr in America. And so on.

Every single one of these people produced, published or patented the idea of a glowing electric filament in a bulb of glass, sometimes containing a vacuum, sometimes nitrogen, and all before Edison, and they did so more or less independently of each other.

This is a very common phenomenon, called simultaneous invention. Almost every invention or discovery results in a dispute about who got there first.

The truth is that the story of the light bulb, far from illustrating the importance of the heroic inventor, turns out to tell the opposite story: of innovation as a gradual, incremental, collective yet inescapably inevitable process. The light bulb emerged inexorably from the combined technologies of the day. It was bound to appear when it did, given the progress of other technologies. It was ripe. Yet still nobody saw it coming. How can innovation be both inevitable and unpredictable?

Take a more recent example: the search engine. This is perhaps the most useful new tool of my lifetime. I use it pretty well every day. I cannot imagine life without it. I get frustrated when it's not available, as for example when I tried to find a book on my shelves that I wanted to re-read when preparing this lecture. In the end I gave up and bought the book again on to my Kindle.

But did I, or anybody else, foresee the immense importance of search in the era of the internet? Did we sit around in the 1980s saying 'if only we could have search engines'? No – no more than people sat around in the 1600s saying 'if only we could have steam engines, we could have an industrial revolution'.

Yet if Sergey Brin had never met Larry Page, we'd still have search engines. There were lots of rivals to Google. The inventors of the search engine, like the inventors of the light bulb, are all entirely dispensable individuals. Re-run the tape of history without all of them and somebody else would have done it.

It is my contention that innovation is the most important unsolved problem in all of human society. We rely on it, but we do not fully understand it, we cannot predict it and we cannot direct it.

It's worth at this point distinguishing between invention, development and commercialisation, but I am taking the word innovation to cover all three stages.

What has this to do with Friedrich Hayek? Quite a lot, I think. In his famous essay on the uses of knowledge in society, Hayek makes the argument that the knowledge required to make society function is dispersed among ordinary people, rather than available centrally and in concentrated form to experts. Towards the end of that essay, he takes to task Joseph Schumpeter, the famous champion of innovation. He's talking about the facts we need to know to determine how best to solve an economic need (Hayek 1945):

> The problem is thus in no way solved if we can show that all the facts, *if* they were known to a single mind ... would uniquely determine the solution; instead we must show how a solution is produced by the interactions of people each of whom possesses only partial knowledge.

Hayek was also fascinated by evolution. Here he is describing the paradox I have just referred to, in regard to evolution rather than economics (Hayek 1973):

> If it were possible to ascertain the particular facts of the past which operated on the selection of the particular forms that emerged, it would provide a complete explanation of the structure of the existing organisms; and similarly, if it were possible to ascertain all the particular facts which will operate on them during some future period, it ought to enable us to predict future development. But, of course, we will never be able to do either.

Technological innovation, like evolution, is a bottom-up phenomenon that emerges by trial and error among the ideas of ordinary people, not a *deus ex machina* that descends upon a few brilliant minds.

We're too creationist about this. We've been telling it wrong for a very long time. We've singled out heroes, and told stories about moments of inspiration that are thoroughly misleading: people jumping out of baths, people being hit on the head by apples, people watching the lids of kettles jump, and so on.

Who invented the computer? The closer you look into it, the harder it is to answer that question and decide between the claims of John von Neumann, Alan Turing, John Mauchly, Presper Eckert, Herman Goldstine, John Vincent Atanasoff, Howard Aiken, Grace Hopper, Charles Babbage and Ada Lovelace, to name just a few. In a real sense, the computer evolved, emerged and invented itself.

Who invented the internet? Everybody and nobody. It evolved. It's the same with the English language: nobody invented it and nobody is in charge. Yet it's certainly man-made. As the philosopher Adam Ferguson said in 1767, there are things that are the result of human action but not the execution of any human design.

Mostly innovation happens by a sort of recombination among ideas, very like the way genetic change happens through recombination of genetic sequences in evolution. As Brian Arthur has argued, every technology is a combination of other technologies, every idea a combination of other ideas. The pill camera came about after a conversation over a garden fence between a gastroenterologist and a guided missile designer.

This incidentally is why the notion that we will run out of ideas or resources, or growth, is so wrong. As I put it in *The Rational Optimist* (Ridley 2011):

> The wonderful thing about knowledge is that it is genuinely limitless. There is not even a theoretical possibility of exhausting the supply of ideas, discoveries and

inventions. This is the biggest cause for my optimism of all. It is a beautiful feature of information systems that they are far vaster than physical systems: the combinatorial vastness of the universe of possible ideas dwarfs the puny universe of physical things. As Paul Romer puts it, the number of different software programs that can be put on one-gigabyte hard disks is 27 million times greater than the number of atoms in the universe.

It follows that innovation is mostly about perspiration, not inspiration, as Edison said. He and his team tried 6,000 different plant materials for the filament of a light bulb before settling on bamboo. To put it another way, turning a discovery or an invention into a workable innovation is far harder than having a new idea in the first place.

Perhaps this explains another regularity in the history of technology: that we overestimate the impact of an innovation in the short run, but we underestimate it in the long run. This is known as Amara's law after a 1960s' computer pioneer.

As with all evolutionary systems, you cannot easily hurry innovation. We cannot invent things before they are ready to be invented. Bad luck Lady Lovelace – you were born a century too soon.

It is surprisingly hard to think of things that could have been invented decades before they actually were. Even wheeled suitcases came at about the right time as airports expanded and lightweight wheels came along.

Moore's Law tells us that improvements in the performance of computers were regular and predictable, yet we could not use that information to jump ahead. Why not? Because each step was necessary for the next one. Innovation moves to the adjacent possible. 'Natura non facit saltus', said Linnaeus, echoing Leibniz. Nature does not jump. And yet, I say again, it's also surprisingly hard to plan, predict or stimulate innovation. Forcing it to happen is hard.

Steve Jobs took a gamble on the idea that computers were ready to become consumer goods and he was right. But when Elizabeth Holmes tried explicitly to emulate his approach (as well as his black turtleneck outfits) with blood diagnostic tests, assuming that innovation would arrive if she demanded it, she ended up presiding over an infamous fraud called Theranos.

And here are two quotations to remind you of just how hopeless experts are at predicting the future of technology:

> There is no reason for any individual to have a computer in his home.
>> Ken Olsen, founder of the Digital Equipment Corporation in 1977

> By 2005 or so, it will become clear that the Internet's impact on the economy has been no greater than the fax machine's.
>> Paul Krugman, Nobel-winning economist in 1998

When I was a child, the future was going to be all about amazing new forms of transport: personal gyrocopters, routine space travel, supersonic airliners. Computers hardly got a mention, and telephones none at all. Yet I've lived through very little change in transport at all. Boeing 747s are still flying the Atlantic; they were designed in the 1960s.

By contrast, for the first half of the twentieth century, transport changed dramatically, communication hardly at all. My grandparents were born before the car or the aeroplane, and died after men landed on the moon, but saw little change in telephones, telegraphs and typewriters during their lives. I've had the opposite experience. So it's just not true that all innovation is speeding up. I have a hunch that the next fifty years are not going to be about computers, as we tend to assume, but about biotech or something else.

How does innovation cause economic growth?

Now, innovation is the source of most economic growth. But how does innovation cause growth? It's mostly about time. Economic growth is the reduction in the time it takes to fulfil a need.

So, to take artificial light as an example again, today it takes you about ⅓ of a second of work on the average wage to earn an hour of light from a single LED bulb. In 1950 it took your grandparents 8 seconds; in 1880, with a paraffin lamp 15 minutes; in 1800 with a tallow candle, 6 hours of work. That reduction leaves you free to spend the extra time earning a different service or good, or relaxing and consuming.

At this point, it's worth saying that there is no longer even a smidgen of possibility that innovation leads to an overall increase in unemployment. To believe that is to ignore not just the evidence of three centuries, but theory as well. It's to think in zero-sum terms of diminishing returns.

Ever since the first threshing machines on farms, people have worried that automation costs jobs. Instead it creates them by freeing people and capital to seek out new ways for people to employ each other.

The big theme of human history has been more and more specialisation in the way we work so we can get more and more diverse in the way we consume. It's a trend that goes into reverse during periods of impoverishment, when people return to self-sufficiency, such as after the fall of Rome, or even during the Great Depression in America, where memoirs are full of stories of families raising chickens and vegetables in the yard. Forcing self-sufficiency on people results in poverty, as Mao Tse Tung vividly demonstrated.

Compared with animals, or with subsistence farmers, most people can exchange a few hours of highly specialised production – a 'job' – for a cornucopia of different foods, goods, experiences, entertainments and travel. We work for each other.

It follows that innovation usually fails if it does not cut the time-cost of acquiring goods and services. That is nuclear power's current problem, and space manufacturing, and renewable energy. Innovations that deliver no new or cheaper services don't spread unless subsidised.

This is also why inventions are often slow to get going; it's not the device or the idea, but the falling cost that helps them kick in and change the world. Hayek is right that the price is everything.

Innovation is as much the mother as the daughter of science. The steam engine led to thermodynamics not vice versa. Social media, the mobile phone, drones, block chain – all owe little to academic discoveries. It's just not true that most innovation begins with scientific research; some does, but a lot doesn't.

So growth is the fruit of innovation. But what is innovation? Why does it happen to us, but not to rabbits and rocks? Why does it happen in some places and at some times, but not in others? And when and why did it start?

My answer to this last question, which I still think is at least half original, to the extent that any idea is original, is that there came a moment in the history of hominins, when for whatever reason they stumbled upon the habit of exchange, and that this was the cause of innovation. This is of course a bit of a circular argument but bear with me. When people began to trade things, ideas could meet and mate, with the result that a sort of collective brain could form, far more powerful than individual brains.

We know that our ancestors had technology without innovation, strange as that sounds. *Homo erectus* made Acheulian hand axes to roughly the same design all over the world for the best part of a million years with little change.

The evidence suggests that Neanderthals, though much more intelligent than *Homo erectus*, did not experience much innovation either: unlike modern people they did not switch to other prey if one food source ran out. They did not engage in exchange either; they used only local materials for tools, whereas even the earliest modern humans often sourced materials from a long way away, almost certainly through trade. I think that's no coincidence: without exchange you get no innovation. In short, what triggered innovation was trade. And trade is about 100,000 years old.

Anthropologists are catching on. In 2011 an important paper from UCL argued that temporary 'outbreaks' of new technology in palaeolithic southern Africa probably have a demographic explanation. That is, when population density rose, it resulted in a spurt of innovation; when population density fell, it resulted in technological regress. And since population density has no such effect in rabbits, this points to exchange and specialisation as the causal link.

Michelle Kline and Rob Boyd (2010) have since produced evidence from Pacific islands that technological complexity of pre-contact fishing tackle on any island correlated with population size and contact with other islands. The most remarkable example is the case of Tasmania, which became an island 10,000 years ago as a result of rising sea levels. Thereafter its isolated population not only failed to acquire new technologies from the mainland, such as the boomerang, but actually regressed, gradually giving up bone tools altogether.

Joe Henrich argues that this shows that technology, because of specialisation, is a collective not an individual phenomenon. It's knowledge held in the cloud. And of course the evidence from the modern world overwhelmingly supports the link between trade, or exchange, and innovation.

My friend Paul Romer deservedly got the Nobel Prize in 2018 for his attempt to tackle the question of how to explain technological change. Here it is necessary to dip into economic theory. David Warsh, in his fascinating history of economics entitled *Knowledge and the Wealth of Nations* (the book I could not find on my shelf), makes the argument that there lurks a contradiction in Adam Smith that has rumbled underground, largely ignored for more than two centuries (Warsh 2006).

Smith's Invisible Hand drives markets towards perfect equilibrium, implying diminishing or flat returns. Smith's pin factory, by contrast, implies disruptive discovery through specialisation and the division of labour, which implies the opposite of diminishing returns – increasing returns. One implies negative feedback, the other positive feedback. Which is it?

In the years that followed Smith, economists such as Ricardo, Mill, Jevons, Walras, Marshall and Keynes largely ignored increasing returns and the pin factory. They focused on the Invisible Hand, more or less explicitly expecting growth to slow as equilibrium was approached. Here's Warsh on John Stuart Mill, for example:

> Mill didn't ignore technical progress altogether. But he didn't try to explain it, either – at least not in economic terms. He simply assumed that it would continue for at least a while longer.

Yet the reverse of diminishing returns kept happening; growth accelerated. And still, specialisation and the growth of knowledge never became a central concern of economics. From time to time the paradox would burst to the surface, to be explained by magical thinking, such as

Marshall's 'spillover' externalities, which Warsh describes as 'a clever device to reconcile increasing returns with the assumption of Invisible Hand perfect competition and still make the mathematics come out right'.

The person who surfaced the issue most bluntly was Allyn Young in 1928, who argued that Smith had missed the point. What went on inside the pin factory was only part of the story of the division of labour: 'The invention of new tools and machinery and new materials and designs involved the division of labor as well' (quoted in Warsh 2006).

Joseph Schumpeter also tried to bring knowledge and technology to the forefront, saying that to do economics without it was like playing Hamlet without the Prince. And he was adamant that growth was potentially infinite, writing (Schumpeter 1942):

> It is one of the safest predictions that in the calculable future we shall live in an embarras de richesse of both foodstuffs and raw materials, giving all the rein to expansion of total output that we shall know what to do with.

But because he wrote in words, rather than formulae, Schumpeter was largely ignored.

Then along comes Robert Solow in 1957 with his startling conclusion that extra land, labour and capital can explain just 15 per cent of growth (Solow 1957). The rest – the 'residual' – must be changing technology. Since he arrives at this conclusion using maths, at last his colleagues take notice.

But in Solow's model, innovation is an external factor, a sort of manna from heaven. As Warsh puts it, 'Like the map of Africa, the Solow model of the sources of growth consisted of bold outlines, with little interior detail and most of the interesting action deliberately left out'. (Incidentally, for me, Warsh's book was an eye opener. How on earth could economists have for so long continued to ignore innovation, the pre-eminent fact of the past two centuries? For that matter how could politicians ignore innovation today? I sit in the House of Lords, admittedly an institution that has defied much innovation for many centuries, but which purports to tackle the big issues of the country, yet I can count on the fingers of one hand the times we have debated how to encourage innovation. How to regulate it we discuss rather more often.)

It was Romer in 1990 who made growth endogenous, who saw that innovation was itself a product; that knowledge is both an input and an output of the economy, and that the key characteristic of new knowledge is that it is both non-rivalrous, that is to say lots of people can share it without using it up, and partially excludable, that is to say whoever gets hold of it first can make money exploiting it, at least for a while. Knowledge is expensive to produce, but then can pay for itself. As Warsh put it,

> People cooked up the new instructions in the hope of making money, then either kept secret some aspects of them, patented them, or used the advantage of their new-found knowledge to keep going forward to create still more new knowledge.

This is a key insight that in my view undermines the view on the left that knowledge is a public good that can only be paid for by the state, and the view on the right that government needs to grant explicit monopolies in the form of patents and copyrights. Set up right, society will generate new knowledge within networks or markets.

Terence Kealey has gone further, arguing that the evidence strongly suggests that private interests will invest in research, and that government doing so instead, on the assumption of a market failure, ends up crowding out such investment. This is not a debate I want to join here, except to say that whether you encourage research by grants, prizes, tax breaks or deregulation, you almost certainly do help innovation.

Picking winners, however, is a mistake. Governments have championed certain new technologies throughout my lifetime, and frankly the record is dismal. Concorde, advanced gas-cooled reactors, interactive television, virtual reality villages, wind turbines, biofuels – the list of losers is long. I have a feeling graphene and electric cars may join that list. The list of winners that government missed is just as long. The internet, mobile phones, social media, vaping, shale gas, gene editing. We're back to the unpredictability of technological change.

Barriers to innovation

I think the recipe for encouraging innovation is terribly simple. Seek out and destroy barriers that get in its way. Because there are always huge vested interests ranged against innovation. As Fredrik Erixon and Bjorn Weigel have pointed out in their book *The Innovation Illusion*, big companies and big public agencies do their best to protect their rent-seeking opportunities; they strive to stifle innovation every way they can (Erixon and Weigel 2016). Let me give two recent examples:

Sir James Dyson invented the bagless vacuum cleaner. The German vacuum industry lobbied Brussels for the power consumption of vacuum cleaners (which were to be regulated to prevent global warming) to be tested in the absence of dust, because if there is dust around, the German devices work less well. In November 2018, Dyson won his case in court, but it took five years. Second, the pharmaceutical industry has lobbied hard – in Brussels and Washington mainly – for the regulation and restriction of vaping devices, to protect its prescribed patches and gums.

As the late Calestous Juma (2016) chronicled in his book *Innovation and Its Enemies*, in the past hansom cab operators in London furiously denounced the introduction of the umbrella. Margarine, invented in France in 1869, was subjected to a decades-long smear campaign (blame Professor Juma for the pun, not me) from the American dairy industry. 'There never was ... a more deliberate and outrageous swindle than this bogus butter business', thundered the New York dairy commission. By the early 1940s, two thirds of states had banned yellow margarine altogether on spurious health grounds.

The National Health Service is another big business that is notorious, as Sir John Bell has recently argued, for its resistance to innovation. It is one of the last health services in the western world to adopt proton beam therapy for cancer. Randox, the leading producer of blood diagnostics based on proteins in the world, is based in the UK. It sells to 145 countries, but struggles to get a foothold in the NHS.

Science too is full of barriers to innovation, such as peer review, and its tendency to punish new ideas that diverge from a cosy consensus. Consider a recent article detailing the long struggle that Robert Moir had to get his hypothesis about Alzheimer's and viruses taken seriously. Or the even longer struggle that Moir's mentor, Barry Marshall, had a generation ago to get the bacterial causes of stomach ulcers considered. Marshall got the Nobel Prize – eventually. But it was uphill work.

The economist Alexander Tabarrok has shown that, by increasing research costs and delaying drug introductions, the Food and Drug Administration (FDA) quite plausibly costs more lives than it saves in the US. Brink Lindsey and Steve Teles (2017) argue in their new book, *The Captured Economy*, that intellectual property, occupational licensing and government favouritism also do much to keep innovators out.

Patents and copyrights, originally intended to encourage innovation, have become far more often ways of defending monopolies against disruption. It is bonkers that, thanks to lobbying from the Disney Corporation, my heirs can earn royalties from my books till 70 years after my death. Let them get a job instead!

Then there is the precautionary principle. This superficially sensible idea – that we should worry about the unintended consequences of innovation – has morphed into a device by which activists prevent life-saving new technologies getting started, even when these are demonstrably safer and better than existing technologies. The precautionary principle (PP), as adopted by the EU, holds the new to a higher standard than the old. E-cigs have to test their vapour for far more chemicals than cigarettes have to, for example. It ignores the risks of existing technologies, defying the concept of harm reduction. Indeed, it essentially argues that you should never do anything for the first time.

Cass Sunstein argues that when taken to an extreme, the precautionary principle is largely meaningless: both action and inaction create some risk to health, leaving little reason to choose between the two. The asymmetric nature of the PP is this: in an imperfect world, standing in the way of an innovation that might do good causes real harm. It's a version of Frédéric Bastiat's argument about the seen and the unseen.

Hostility to innovation in the European Commission and Parliament, by the way, is the biggest reason I voted Leave in 2016. Having seen the Commission and Parliament set their faces against vaping, against fracking, against genetic modification, against bagless vacuum cleaners, often on the most spurious of grounds and often at the behest of corporate lobbies for incumbent interests; having seen the way the EU placed obstacles in the way of digital start-ups, leaving Europe in the slow lane of the digital revolution, and with no digital giants to rival Google, Facebook or Amazon; and having watched the EU's entrenching of an extreme version of the precautionary principle in the Lisbon Treaty itself, I am really worried that this continent won't be able to grow in the future.

In 2016, BusinessEurope produced a long catalogue of cases in which EU regulation had affected innovation. The list includes two cases where regulation stimulated innovation (waste policies and sustainable mobility), but far more where it hampered change by introducing legal uncertainty, inconsistency with other regulations, technology-prescriptive rules, burdensome packaging requirements, high compliance costs or excessive precaution. For example, the EU medical devices directive has greatly increased the cost and reduced the supply of new medical devices.

What Britain needs to adopt in the wake of Brexit is the innovation principle[1] to balance the precautionary principle. This was proposed by the European Risk Forum.[2] In essence, it says: examine every policy for the impact it could have on innovation, and if you find evidence that the policy is going to impede it, then rethink it.

Twenty-two chief executives from some of the world's more innovative companies signed a letter to Jean-Claude Juncker in 2014 asking him to adopt the innovation principle, and the Dutch Prime Minister, Mark Rutte, endorsed

1   Innovation Principle. European Risk Forum (http://www.riskforum.eu/ innovation-principle.html).

2   The Innovation Principle – Overview. European Risk Forum (http://www .riskforum.eu/uploads/2/5/7/1/25710097/innovation_principle_one_pag er_5_march_2015.pdf).

it during his country's presidency of the EU in 2016.[3] That fell on deaf ears, of course.

So my message is that because innovation is a bottom-up evolutionary process deriving from dispersed knowledge, instead of messing around trying to find a magic way to create innovation, government should focus on removing things that stop it.

As long ago as 1662 William Petty, one of the pioneers of economics, pointed out in his treatise on taxes and contributions that:

> when a new invention is first propounded in the beginning every man objects and the poor inventor runs the gantloop of all petulant wits, every man finding his several flaw, no man approving it unless mended according to his own device. Now, not one of a hundred outlives this torture, and those that do are at length so changed by the various contrivances of others, that not any one man can pretend to the invention of the whole, nor well agree about their respective share in the parts.

Today, this is more true than ever. Innovation is a mysterious and under-appreciated process that we discuss too rarely, hamper too much and value too little.

---

3   Toespraak van minister-president Rutte bij het Business Europe Day 'Reform to Perform' event, 3 March 2016 (https://www.rijksoverheid.nl/documenten/toespraken/2016/03/03/speech-by-prime-minister-rutte-at-the-businesseurope-day-reform-to-perform-event).

References

Erixon, F. and Weigel, B. (2016) *The Innovation Illusion: How So Little Is Created by So Many Working So Hard*. Yale University Press.

Hayek, F. A. (1945) The use of knowledge in society. *American Economic Review* 35(4): 519–30.

Hayek, F. A. (1973) *Law, Legislation and Liberty*, Vol. 1: *Rules and Order*. London: Routledge and Kegan Paul.

Juma, C. (2016) *Innovation and Its Enemies: Why People Resist New Technologies*. Oxford University Press.

Kline, M. A. and Boyd, R. (2010) Population size predicts technological complexity in Oceania. *Proceedings of the Royal Society* B: *Biological Sciences* 277(1693): 2559–64.

Lindsey, B. and Teles, S. (2017) *The Captured Economy: How the Powerful Become Richer, Slow Down Growth, and Increase Inequality*. Oxford University Press.

Petty, W. (1662) *A Treatise of Taxes and Contributions*. London: N. Brooke.

Ridley, M. (2011) *The Rational Optimist: How Prosperity Evolves*. London: 4th Estate.

Schumpeter, J. (1942) *Capitalism, Socialism and Democracy*. New York: Harper & Brothers.

Solow, R. M. (1957) Technical change and the aggregate production function. *Review of Economics and Statistics* 39(3): 312–20.

Warsh, D. (2006) *Knowledge and the Wealth of Nations: A Story of Economic Discovery*. New York: W. W. Norton and Company.

2 QUESTIONS AND DISCUSSION

CHARLES AMOS: Which one piece of specific regulation would you get rid of in order to provoke the most innovation, in your view?

MATT RIDLEY: Probably the precautionary principle, or rather, I would balance it with the innovation principle. I would tone it down, because I think it is genuinely causing real problems. So, for example, on genetically modified foods, we now know that we've missed out on significant improvements, not just in the economics of farming but in the ecology of farming, because they have reduced chemical use throughout the world. Yet, they're unavailable in Europe, and we've missed out on that, so that would be the one that I would go for.

JULIO ALEJANDRO: I work with Liberland, Bitnation, a number of artificial intelligence, blockchain and 'intentional communities' like the Seasteading Institute. There have been a number of innovations within financial, commercial, ideas transactions and exchanges, but little has been done within centralised institutions such as governments, but also a physical place where individuals would be able to associate with each other. That's what we call an intentional community, also called a private city, or a charter city, a smart city. Would you think that that could be a new future of evolution, rather than from the digital side, but actually within the physical side of how to free people to interact with each other rather than creating digital transactions as with blockchain or artificial intelligence predictability?

MATT RIDLEY: It's an interesting point. Paul Romer, of course, is the champion of the idea of a charter city, that somewhere in the world you should go to a poor country and say, 'Can we have a piece of your land and can we make a free-trade city in it and see if it works, just to set up a new Hong Kong?' as it were. And we've got the examples of Hong Kong and Singapore, two incredibly successful economies over the last 60 or 70 years because of free trade and because of letting people get on with things.

I think it's a nice idea, but I don't think it's ever going to happen because, when push comes to shove, no country is going to hand over a chunk of their territory for this to happen. At one point, Paul had the idea that he could do this at Guantanamo Bay, which sounded to me quite a good idea.

The founder of PayPal, Peter Thiel, makes the point that one of the reasons most innovation in the last ten years or so has been in the digital economy rather than the physical economy is because digital innovation is permissionless and physical stuff is not. We've essentially not got around to putting barriers in the way of innovation with bits. All our barriers are about innovation with atoms.

Of course, that's changing. Governments are starting to crack down on bits, as it were, quite fast at the moment, but I think that's an interesting point. We think of innovation, at the moment, as being very much a digital thing: artificial intelligence, blockchain, social media, all these kinds of things, and for the last generation, that's been true. But maybe that's because we've made it harder to innovate in the physical world. That's not to say there's been no innovation in the physical world. There has been quite a lot.

JOHN WILDEN: Particularly for the young people present, can you just give, say, a couple of examples from your own really quite dense scientific experience – I know Cold Harbor and other places – where you actually think innovation can be quite smooth and can translate quite quickly? Just for encouragement.

MATT RIDLEY: An example of an innovation that was or could be smoothly introduced. It depends what you mean by smoothly, but I used vaping and electronic cigarettes quite a lot in my talk as a case history, and it's a very interesting question as to why more people vape in the UK than in any other European country by about two and a half times, and why vaping is still banned in Australia but not here. Why vaping is catching up in America, but Britain is way ahead. It's got a diverse vaping industry. A lot more smokers have taken it up. Smoking rates are falling faster in the UK. In Japan, they've gone for a different technology, heat-not-burn cigarettes, and it's still pretty well illegal to take electronic cigarettes into Japan. I trace it back to a lucky accident, that early in the coalition government, David Halpern, head of the 'Nudge Unit', bumped into his old friend Rory Sutherland, the advertising executive, who was an early adopter of electronic cigarettes, and gave David Halpern a quick seminar on what these things were, and Halpern thought, 'That's interesting. These could actually help reduce smoking, rather than make the problem worse'.

He wrote a memo to David Cameron – everybody's called David in this story – the gist of which was 'when the public health experts come through the door and tell you to ban this thing, resist them, because this might be a good technology, not a bad technology'.

But then it got tangled up in the Tobacco Products Directive from the European Union, which banned advertising, and which slowed down the rate of smoking cessation in this country, etc. So, there have been hurdles, but that would be one example.

Another would be mitochondrial replacement therapy in the UK, again a superb piece of science dealing with a particularly rare disease. It came to parliament. We had a huge debate in both houses. Both houses passed it overwhelmingly. It went ahead. It then took a little longer to get going, because of various technical problems, but not because anyone was against it. So, it can be done.

MALE SPEAKER: How would you respond to genetic enhancement potentially limiting human freedom in the future?

MATT RIDLEY: Limiting human freedom through genetic engineering, what's the risk of that? What's the prospect of that? Well, so far, reproductive and genetic technologies have been liberating. Think about the impact of in vitro fertilisation, test tube babies. It was thought this was going to be a tool for central-planning autocrats who wanted to produce supermen. People were really, really worried in the 60s and 70s that, if in vitro fertilisation caught on and became easy to do, it would be used by people to basically make sure that everybody was the child of the supreme leader of the country, etc.

In fact, it had exactly the opposite effect. It enabled people who couldn't have children to have their own children. It liberated them. And the demand for Nobel Prize–winning sperm turned out to be extremely small, because people don't want Nobel Prize–winning fathers for their children, they want their own children. You know, they want children like them. So, I think the same will happen if we get anywhere close to designer baby-type technologies.

If you can go into a clinic in some years' time and be offered 46 genetic tweaks to your unborn child that will make it slightly more musical, slightly more intelligent, slightly better at sports or something, the 'slightly' is key. We now know that these factors come from huge numbers of genes, each with a very small effect, so you're probably going to have to choose about a thousand changes before you can make noticeable differences in these respects, and you don't know what the unintended consequences are. So, I just don't see it catching on.

But if you did it, I suspect the demand would be for people to get rid of problems, as it is now, with pre-implantation genetic screening. To get rid of disease risks, not to improve and enhance. So, I'm relatively relaxed about how people are going to use these technologies, certainly in terms of limiting human freedom.

ROBERT COBBOLD: I'm a huge fan of the idea that we need to remove barriers to innovation, and I wonder if we need to take this insight all the way down into the realm of human consciousness, which evolves through a series of recognisable stages? One of the key insights of Integral Theory is that we've gone from a traditional stage of duty and those values, to a modernist stage of economic growth and secular values, to a postmodern stage. How can we take that insight into our own personalities? How can we remove barriers to innovation in our own evolution, as much as the evolution of technology?

MATT RIDLEY: On the whole, I haven't really thought about that, I have to admit, and I think that the amount of cultural and economic and technological evolution we can do is now so overwhelmingly large and fast that I'm not too worried about changing our biology. We do, of course, change our biology. We've adapted to modern living.

There's a fascinating book just coming out from Richard Wrangham about how we're a domesticated species. We've learned to gather in large groups and not attack each other, which chimpanzees can't do. This room would be chaos if we were chimpanzees. That's through a form of selection, of evolution.

I genuinely think that we have passed the buck to technological evolution, mostly, and that there's no point messing around by trying to encourage biological evolution in our species, because it's so slow and inadequate as a way of changing.

JONATHAN CLARK: Shall we, then, abolish the British Academy and the Royal Society, prestigious bodies that have no other function than to be protectionist restraints on innovation?

MATT RIDLEY: Well, since neither have elected me to their membership, I quite agree. [Laughter]

LUCY NEVILLE-ROLFE: I want you to be Chancellor for a moment, and tell us what you think about innovation incentives, things like R&D tax credits, given what you've said about the diffuse process of innovation.

MALE SPEAKER: My question is actually similar. A couple of years ago, the government undertook a Patient Capital Review. My question is, how much do you think the inability to have patient investors restrains innovation?

MATT RIDLEY: Well, I think my answers to Lucy's question and the second question are probably fairly similar, inasmuch as I like anything that encourages research and development as long as it's not trying to pick winners and specifically singling ones out, and I worry about the catapults and things in that respect. Although they're not too bad there. But I do think that in this country we are chronically bad at the second stage, the patient capital, the build-up, the commercialisation. And we still think of innovation as invention-discovery, and actually, that's the 1 per cent inspiration that Edison talked about, not the 99 per cent perspiration.

Incentives to develop businesses out of these ideas are probably where the British focus needs to be to get over our inherent problems in that respect. So, I'm all for patient capital, and things like Entrepreneurs' Relief and EIS [Enterprise Investment Scheme] actually did have a big impact.

The UK start-up ecosystem is actually pretty spectacular: since 2010, 600,000 start-ups a year, more than the rest of the European Union combined, much more than in the preceding ten years. Now, some of those are probably not very good, but Entrepreneurs' Relief and EIS have encouraged much more of that second-stage stuff, and we need to build on that and get it to keep working later.

FEMALE SPEAKER: You suggested that you used hostility to innovation and the precautionary principle as a reason for voting leave, but my question is, given the current climate of Brexit negotiations, and particularly May's newly drafted deal, how plausible will it be for the UK to embrace innovation after leaving the EU?

MATT RIDLEY: That brings me onto how to encourage innovation outside the EU, if we are indeed outside the EU, and the high alignment that is apparently in the deal that we are about to hear about from the steps of Downing Street.

A high degree of alignment on goods in particular will make it very hard to do anything differently. Just to take gene editing, this technology that the rest of the world is saying doesn't need heavy and specific regulation and that the European Court has ruled does need heavy and specific regulation, and which, therefore, is bailing out of this country as fast as it can to Canada and other places. I'm talking about gene editing in agriculture. It'll be different when it comes to gene editing in medicine.

One of the things I was hoping we could do, if we left, was say, 'Right. Well, in that case, we'll recognise that it needs less regulation and can be fast-tracked into production'. It will be hard to embrace this aspect of Brexit with this deal, I can't deny that.

JOHN STRAFFORD: Hayek wrote in *The Road to Serfdom* that when you have regulation upon regulation upon regulation, the end of the road is the totalitarian state, tyranny and dictatorship. I can see the end of the road in this country and in Europe. How can ordinary people use innovation to reverse that direction of travel?

MATT RIDLEY: How do we use innovation to get around the drift towards a totalitarian state? Well, isn't it fascinating how we thought that the technologies that were coming along, starting with the fax machine and the mobile phone and going into the internet, were going to be incredibly liberating for the individual and were going to undermine the basis of state control of us?

Twenty years ago, we were so idealistic about this. It's almost hard to remember now, and the state has fought back and has found ways of using these technologies, whether it's through fake news or through surveillance, or whatever, to make us just as much under their thumb as before, perhaps more in some cases.

These things go in waves, though, and I do think that there will be opportunities to dissolve the power of totalitarians through technology, and on the whole the genie is out of the bottle. It would be relatively hard to set up an absolutely totalitarian state in a Western democracy, but it's proved surprisingly easy in some other countries in recent years, I have to say, and that's taken me by surprise.

MALE SPEAKER: I want to go back to something you spoke about earlier in your talk, about the FDA and about how potentially it has caused more harm than good through, essentially, picking winners, with a twenty-year process of getting approved. Obviously, it seems to me, the point of that is to prevent a snake oil salesman selling you a cabbage pill that he claims will cure your cancer. So, I want to ask, what do you think is the best way to balance an ex ante system of testing with an ex post system of specifically targeting fraudsters? Alternatively, do you think those kinds of fears are overblown?

MATT RIDLEY: I don't feel I'm enough of an expert on the FDA and medical regulation to give you a very full answer here. Clearly, we don't want another Thalidomide. We need to be testing things before they get put into human beings, etc. But we must, at the same time, encourage new ideas and new technologies to come forward. I don't feel we've got the balance right at the moment.

If you look at what drug companies spend the monopoly profits they get out of patents on, it's not necessarily R&D. It's basically marketing, a lot of it, so it's reinforcing the monopoly as well. I think one needs to address that question.

There are things like allowing orphan drugs to be tested in different conditions; allowing people who are dying to try drugs so that they can contribute knowledge about the safety of medicines, and so on; there are all sorts of imaginative ways that can be tried.

ROBERT AFIA: Competition, I would have thought, is a big generator of innovation. So, encourage competition and would you not get more innovation?

MATT RIDLEY: Competition, absolutely, but I sometimes think that free-market people talk about competition too much, and cooperation too little. Actually, what goes on vertically within a market is cooperation between the buyer and the seller, whereas the horizontal stuff between two sellers competing is very important, it's a crucial part of it, but I feel it puts people off if we talk about that too much and don't talk about the collaboration that can come from the way people work for each other in these sorts of worlds.

Competing with yourself to deliver a better product to your customer is just as important as competing with someone else, I think.

3 INNOVATION, GROWTH AND POSSIBLE FUTURES

Stephen Davies

Introduction

In the last few years there has been a realisation of how central innovation is to the modern world. It is innovation that produces its distinctive features, above all sustained intensive growth, and makes our world so radically different from that of our ancestors. This is the main theme for example of Deirdre McCloskey's magnum opus in (so far) three parts, which goes so far as to argue that we should stop using the term 'capitalism' and simply speak of innovation and what it requires. I have also made a similar point myself, although I disagree slightly with McCloskey over how to explain the sudden increase in the pace and intensity of innovation in the last two hundred and fifty years (McCloskey 2007, 2010, 2017; Davies 2019). The emphasis on innovation as the key to understanding modernity is, however, widespread, as this lecture by Matt Ridley shows. Given that recognised fact, understanding what innovation is, where it comes from, why it has been much less common historically than in the last two hundred years, and how it can be hindered or even stopped, is a matter of great importance.

At one time there were many economic theories that tried to explain the phenomenon of economic growth and identify a fundamental cause for the kind of growth the world has seen since around 1750. These ranged from the impact of trade and the division of labour together with the extent of the market (Adam Smith) to the active role of governments, and national governments in particular, in stimulating invention (many authors). However, over the last two decades or so a consensus has emerged that the economist who got the correct answer was Schumpeter: it is entrepreneurship, innovation and the gale of creative destruction that economists now point to as the source of genuine wealth-creating and increasing growth.

Ridley's lecture fits into the continuing discussion and addresses the questions set out earlier. In particular, he is concerned with the sources of innovation and with its social basis, the kinds of social relations that create innovation and without which it cannot happen. This leads to the point of how certain trends in the contemporary world are dangerous and should be deprecated and resisted because they are potentially fatal for the kind of sustained innovation that has brought about the unparalleled wealth and comfort of the modern world. In his lecture he makes a number of points that bear emphasis and expansion about the social nature and basis of innovation. When drawn out and explored these lead to radical and perhaps surprising conclusions about central aspects of the current world economy. This becomes even more the case when his analysis is placed into a chronologically longer and geographically wider historical perspective. At the same time there are arguments against his position that need to be addressed, and in at least one case we can say that the jury is still out, even though I share his judgement as to what the verdict of history will finally be.

The Hayek Lecture's main arguments

The Hayek Lecture sets out several arguments. The central one is that innovation is the product not of heroic visionaries or outstanding and rare individuals, but of large numbers of ordinary, enquiring and enterprising people and the interactions between them. Thus, it rejects the idea Ayn Rand expressed in *The Fountainhead*: that progress and innovation come from Promethean individuals, with the rest of humanity eventually following them and benefitting from their creativity. Instead, innovation is a social phenomenon, with any particular innovation having many parents and originators, most of them forgotten or even unknown. What matters is the social framework of trade and the free exchange of both goods and ideas among people. Ridley powerfully makes the point that where trade, exchange and contact with the rest of the world are reduced or absent, innovation tends not to happen and regression can actually take place. The classic historical example of this is the fate of Western Europe in the aftermath of the collapse of the West Roman Empire and the disruption of Mediterranean sea routes by the Arab conquests. As Bryan Ward-Perkins (2006) has shown, the result was a decline in trade, a disastrous reduction in wealth and production and the systematic loss of a whole range of technologies (one of which, Roman concrete, has only just been rediscovered[1]).

Ridley's second argument, which follows from this, is that innovation and creativity are the product of voluntary human interaction. This means that it is futile and even counterproductive to try and plan it or encourage it by deliberate political action – a point Terence Kealey (1996) has made very powerfully. It also means that restraining human interaction and exchange will hamper or even prevent innovation. As he points out, the difficult thing in the process of innovation is not so much the generation of the original idea or vision (though that is difficult enough) but the conversion of the vision into a useful and practical innovation that brings about an increase in wealth and human well-being. It is that process of tinkering, experimentation and marginal improvement that requires the free interaction of millions of people and the unhindered exchange of not just ideas, but products, goods and services.

The way in which this brings about innovation and creativity can be seen very clearly in fields such as music and cuisine. Here, interaction and trade between people lead to experimentation and the development of new kinds of cuisine and forms of music. An important aspect of this is the appearance of cultural hybrids that combine knowledge and insight from different cultures and parts of the world. For example, the Indian cuisine that most British

---

1   For the recent rediscovery of the secret of Roman concrete, see https://unews.utah.edu/roman-concrete/.

people are familiar with is actually Mughlai cooking, the cuisine of the Mughals, which combined indigenous Indian techniques and ingredients with others drawn from the Mughals' original homeland of Central Asia (the use of yoghurt for example) and yet others brought to India by Arab traders and the Portuguese (such as the potato, the tomato and the chilli pepper). One very important conclusion to draw is that it is completely wrong to believe that global trade is producing a world of cultural uniformity – in fact it creates the exact opposite, more diversity and variety, along with greater innovation (Cowen 2004).

A key argument of the lecture is that innovation leads to economic growth and increased productivity (and hence greater wealth) because it frees up time, the ultimate scarce resource, to be used for other activity and hence more output. Here I would qualify the argument slightly. Innovation does indeed lead to greater efficiency and intensity in the use of time but it does the same for all resources, including raw materials of all kinds. The one possible exception to that rule is energy, but even that is not true in the long run, as we shall see later. This is why the long-run trend over the last three centuries has been for the real cost of raw materials to decline, indicating that they are actually more abundant despite being 'used up'. The reason is the greater intensity of use, which means for example that a product that required a kilo of copper fifty years ago will now only require a fraction of that or even none, with the copper now replaced by a substitute such as glass. One important conclusion is that concern about automation destroying paid work is misplaced, as it has been for over two hundred years. However, this does not mean that other concerns about innovation should not be considered, as we shall see.

The final main argument of the lecture is the one that I have some disagreement with and this is the point where greater historical perspective can actually strengthen the argument and make it better founded, as well as making it clearer exactly what kinds of threats to innovation we now face. The argument is that particular innovations cannot happen until the time is ripe, in the sense that a number of other innovations have to take place first before the later one becomes possible. Moreover, when those earlier innovations have happened the need for other innovations then becomes acute in a way that it was not before and this leads to lots of experimentation and exploration of how to produce them. An example would be the telephone, which was not possible until electrical technology had become sufficiently developed. Once it was, the acute need for an effective means of long-distance spoken communication in the increasingly urbanised and globalised world of the later nineteenth century meant that many people were working on a means of doing this with a constant exchange of ideas and techniques – Alexander Graham Bell was only one of many. Ridley goes so far as to discount the phenomenon of innovations that could have occurred at any time until someone had the vision, arguing that the wheeled suitcase, often given as an example of an innovation that could have happened long before it did, could not have been introduced until certain other innovations had happened.

This argument has a number of far-reaching implications. The first is that innovation is cumulative – this is one reason why the frequency of innovations has accelerated over time and the time for the diffusion of innovations has shrunk. The second is that the process of innovation is gradual and continuous, as long as the preconditions of enough people and sufficient unhindered trade and exchange of ideas are in place. The third and major set of implications is historical. If innovation is what explains the modern (post-1750) world with its sustained growth and rising living standards, and if innovation is indeed the result of a long-run cumulative process in which each innovation rests on ones previously made, without which they could not come about, then several things follow. It means that the modern world of sustained intensive growth could not have happened before it actually did. The change after the middle of the eighteenth century was therefore a take-off (to use Walt Rustow's expression) that became possible only once a critical level of innovation, population and interconnections between different parts of the world had been reached. Finally, this means that the modern world was in some sense inevitable so long as the processes of trade and exchange that produce innovation had been allowed to continue for long enough.

There is a lot of truth in this model. In particular it is clearly true that certain specific innovations depend upon other ones being made earlier – or indeed at the same time. One of the things that is literally unknowable is the list of innovations that have not happened because those preconditions have not yet been met or the perceived need for them has not yet become manifest. We can only talk about the ones that have happened. However, this picture needs to be severely qualified. The list of innovations that could have happened earlier than they did may be longer than Ridley supposes. It is true for example that the container ship required certain prior technological breakthroughs and innovations in organisation and management, but those preconditions were met several decades before the container ship was actually introduced. There are significant lags in other words. However, that is not the main qualification that needs to be made.

The real problem is that there is much evidence to hand that the speeding up and sustaining of innovation that we call modernity could have started some time before it did. If we look at the long course of human history, what is striking is how little things change when one considers, for example, the patterns and structures of everyday life or the standards of living of the great majority of people. However, there are repeated episodes in which we see bursts of innovation and the first signs of sustained intensive growth, typically in a specific part of the planet (Goldstone 2002). These episodes correlate with three other things: stable government over a large part of the planet's surface, open intellectual enquiry and discussion, and a higher level of trade and exchange, including the appearance of relatively sophisticated forms of finance. There was one such episode in the lands around the Mediterranean in the second century, for example, another in parts of the Middle East in the later eighth and early ninth century, another in parts of Western Europe in the twelfth century. All of these episodes saw major innovations and discoveries. They did not last, however, as things reverted to the historical norm of relative stasis and in many cases the technologies and innovations that were produced were subsequently forgotten and lost. (An example of this was the use of a form of battery for electroplating, invented in the episode that happened under the Abbasids in Baghdad.)

The biggest and most significant episode of this kind took place in China during the twelfth and thirteenth centuries, under the remarkable Song dynasty. The Song, unlike previous and subsequent dynasties, deliberately encouraged trade and commerce and relaxed the extensive controls on the Chinese population that were a traditional part of China's imperial governance. The result was an outburst of new ideas and technologies, leading to the most significant episode of growth anywhere in the world before the eighteenth century. By the later years of the dynasty, in the thirteenth century, China had a level of technical development and knowledge that was the same as that reached by Western Europe in the early to mid eighteenth century. What this demonstrates is that had the episode of innovative dynamism continued, we would now no doubt be speaking of an industrial revolution of the thirteenth century in China rather than a British one in the eighteenth century. (We would also be far wealthier, assuming that in this counterfactual, growth and innovation had continued since then (Edwards 2013).) So why did this not happen?

Historical barriers to innovation

The answer, I believe, is one that means we cannot believe that the breakthrough into sustained innovation that did happen in the eighteenth century was somehow inevitable, or the conclusion to a long process of cumulative discovery. Rather it is the one case where the forces and factors that had brought earlier episodes to an end were unable to do so again. The reality is this: innovation is indeed the natural and inevitable result of trade and exchange among ordinary people, but there are powerful forces that work against that and limit innovation. Historically, these have proved stronger until recently. These forces are also natural in the sense that like innovation they arise from commonly found human interactions. There are two kinds of force or structure at play here.

The first are what we may call the spontaneous insurance relations and social institutions that human societies have typically produced. The overwhelming reality of life for almost all of our ancestors was that they lived in a Malthusian world, a world of severe scarcity. In this world, because of the lack of sustained innovation and sometimes for other, structural reasons such as low population and low population density, it was very difficult to increase the intensity and efficiency with which resources were used. Generally speaking, over the medium to longer term, output of all kinds grew at the same rate as or even slightly slower than human population. There were occasional windfall gains but these were step changes, not part of a continuous upward slope of production relative to population. The result was that living standards did not rise and for most of history the overwhelming majority lived at the edge of subsistence. One almost universal response was for people to develop institutions, rules, norms and practices that provided security against contingencies and in particular protected people against the effects of change, whether natural or the result of human action. These included things like rules for the sharing of access to key resources such as seeds or tools or the rotation of access to land (as in the medieval European open field system). It also included prohibitions on practices such as buying goods outside strictly limited markets with a view to reselling them at a higher price in the market or elsewhere, and rules that set prices of all kinds (including wages) according to a normative 'just price' which was typically the traditional one. The intention was to protect people against unexpected change and chance and also to prevent people from doing significantly better than their fellows (this didn't stop them trying of course – the point is that doing so was disapproved of and made difficult). The main aim, however, was to make life, and particularly economic life, more predictable and stable and to minimise the effects of change.

These institutions and practices, which were found in varying forms in almost all pre-modern societies, are now commonly referred to as the 'moral economy', a term invented by the historian E. P. Thompson (1991) and applied more widely by the anthropologist James Scott (1976). The tragic paradox is that while they were a response to the conditions of the Malthusian world, they hindered or outright prevented the kind of sustained innovation that leads to escape from the Malthusian cage. This was an inevitable result, given that, as said above, the central aim of these norms, institutions and practices was to minimise change and its effects. It is important to realise that most of the institutions of the moral economy were as much the spontaneous outcome of social interaction as the kind of trades and exchange that led to innovation. This was because both kinds of activity reflected deep-seated features of human nature and motivation. The desire to 'truck, barter and exchange' as Adam Smith put it, derives from the impulse to improve one's condition by peaceful exchange and, crucially, to try something new. However, many human beings are fearful of change, often historically for good reason. Moreover, change, even if it can be objectively shown to have led to improved conditions, is often experienced and perceived as a loss rather than a gain. So spontaneous human interaction does not only lead to innovation, it also leads to responses and actions that work to limit or prevent change and innovation, and this is another powerful feature of human societies.

However, that by itself is probably not enough to explain the way that episodes of intense innovation such as Song China or the Abbasid Middle East came to peter out. Episodes of that kind brought significant benefits in the shape of higher wealth and incomes, but they also brought disruptive change (which was intimately connected to the economic benefits) and this certainly led to a social reaction against the innovations. Nevertheless, we should notice that some of the moral economy's rules and institutions (such as laws against reselling, or guilds that controlled access to trades) involved the use of political power to enforce them. This brings us to the second factor that historically checked innovation, the role of ruling classes and privileged elites.

In the world of Malthusian scarcity there was a second response to the situation of slow to non-existent growth of the 'pie' of production relative to population besides spontaneous social insurance (moral economy). This was predation, acquiring resources from other people not by trade and exchange but through the use of force or fraud. Historically production and exchange on the one hand and predation on the other are the two ways of acquiring income and resources. This means that in every society there are two broad sets of social classes, the productive or 'industrious' classes (as they were once called), and the idle or exploitative classes. The latter control what we may call the means of predation – deadly force and systematic obfuscation. In other words, they are the ruling classes, who ultimately live off not production and exchange but rents extracted from the productive classes (Rustow 1980). (They often do own productive assets, particularly land, but this is a consequence of their controlling deadly force, not a cause as Marx thought). Ruling classes that are purely or excessively predatory do not last long, however. The more astute only extract as much as will allow the productive classes to continue to live and work. They also provide a range of so-called public goods that make peaceful trade and production easier (and so create larger and more stable rents for themselves). The most prominent are protection against other outside predators and against internal violence and predation, together with a means of settling disputes peacefully (so external defence and a legal system), but we can also include a stable currency and things such as uniform weights and measures and free exchange within the territory they control.

Ruling classes by their nature have a mixed view of innovation and the economic growth it creates. On the one hand this is welcome: it creates more wealth for them to tax, and rents that they can spend on things such as palaces, impressive public works and lavish living (and above all on their favourite pastime, wars). However, it is also a threat to them. They are at the top of the existing social hierarchy so why should they welcome change, particularly if their position is insecure? In addition, innovation and the greater wealth it brings to ordinary people and members of the productive classes weaken the ruling classes' control over them and give them greater autonomy and freedom of action. This is why throughout history ruling groups have often supported the anti-innovation institutions of the moral economy by enforcing their norms and rules through courts or by measures such as statutory privileges given to institutions such as guilds. This means deliberately preventing technological or business or financial innovations. Here another factor comes into play: those who have succeeded in the world of voluntary production and exchange and thereby acquired wealth often fear that they will lose that wealth to ambitious younger upstarts and so they turn to the political power, the ruling classes, to protect their own position and entrench it against further change. In the most extreme cases, ruling groups deliberately and systematically stop or reverse innovation.

We can see these other forces at work in all of the previous episodes of innovation but particularly in the Chinese case. There the Song dynasty was overthrown and China conquered in 1276 – by the Mongols. This by itself did not bring an end to the dynamism of Chinese society as the Mongol Yuan dynasty did not make major institutional changes and was also increasingly ineffective. The subsequent Han Chinese dynasty, the Ming, which came to power in 1368 in the person of the Hongwu emperor, reacted to the Mongol conquest by deliberately reversing the policy of the Song and seeking to reduce the commercialisation of Chinese society and to arrest or even roll back innovation of all kinds. The most dramatic example of the latter was the ban on building ships that could sail long distances out of sight of land, which came into effect towards the end of the fifteenth century. Special privileges were given to merchant cartels, with the deliberate aim of stabilising the Chinese economy and society, i.e. limiting innovation. Towards the end of the dynasty, incapacity on the part of the last Ming emperors meant that many of these rules were not enforced and China became once again a very dynamic and mercantile society, but in 1645 the Manchus conquered China and founded the Qing dynasty. The first four Qing emperors were able and conscientious rulers and they restored the earlier policy of the Ming in this regard.

So although innovation is indeed produced by the interaction of ordinary people through the institutions of trade and exchange, and although many innovations do require other innovations to have been made previously before they become possible (so giving the innovative process a cumulative quality), it does not follow that the explosion of innovation that we call modernity was inevitable and could not have happened earlier than it did. The evidence suggests that although almost certainly particular factors had to be in place or reach a critical level before modern innovation could happen, those conditions had been met long before the eighteenth century. Moreover, the key question is that of why the innovative spurt that began in northwestern Europe in the eighteenth century did not fade away like earlier ones but was sustained and indeed accelerated. In that case the force of innovation was able to overcome the social institutions and ruling classes that had choked off sustained innovation in earlier periods. Why was this?

Explaining Europe's take-off

If Ridley's account of innovation and the innovative process is correct (which I think it is) then that itself gives us ideas as to what the answer to that question might be. In broad terms it is that social interactions and relations based upon trade and exchange became more powerful and widespread than those based upon power and also social institutions that reflected a fear of change. Societies went from being predominantly *neophobic* to predominantly *neophiliac*.

There were three specific changes. Firstly some ruling classes (or more accurately enough members of some ruling classes to make a difference) became supportive of innovation and employed political power to assist it by sweeping away social and legal barriers to it (Mokyr 2011, 2018). Secondly there was the emergence of coalitions of social interests that were aware that they gained from innovation and voluntary action. Between roughly 1770 and 1860 they were engaged in an often fierce political and social/cultural conflict with a coalition of interests that opposed innovations and the changes they brought – this second group included both some elites and members of the lower classes, particularly peasants and traditional artisans. In most places it was the forces that favoured innovation that triumphed (although they disagreed among themselves over what led to it and how to encourage it while controlling it). Thirdly there was a cultural shift in which innovation and enterprise came to be admired and emulated, rather than being feared and deprecated (McCloskey 2007, 2010, 2017). (There are several theories as to why these three things came to be strong enough to overcome the countervailing forces when and where they did, but we do not have space to explore those here.)

This is far from bringing the argument to an end, however. In the first place it raises the big question of whether the process of innovation that Ridley identifies is as beneficial as he thinks it is – there are many who disagree with him. More seriously, we must ask whether this time it really is different. Will the sustained and accelerating innovation we have seen for the last two hundred years or so continue, perhaps to the point of a so-called singularity after which things will swiftly become so different that we cannot even imagine or describe what they will be like? Alternatively, are there reasons to think that the emphasis on innovation is overblown and that we are only living in the longest and most dramatic episode of innovation yet, which will end and fade away like all the others? Perhaps most pressingly, could we accidentally and unintentionally recreate the conditions and incentives that applied for most of human history and so bring innovation to an end that way?

Arguments against innovation

The first question is actually the easiest to deal with in some ways. Ever since the very start of modernity there have been people who have decried innovation and particularly technological innovation. One common theme is a focus on the costs of creative destruction (the destruction part such as the disappearance of livelihoods and occupations because of innovation) while ignoring the creative part (the new and different products, occupations and ways of living that appear as a result of those innovations). The more profound argument is that there is something inherently wrong with the process of sustained innovation and the world it has created. This position – which has been articulated by a series of authors, including John Ruskin and William Morris, as well as contemporary primitivists and deep ecologists such as John Zerzan and the 'Unabomber' Ted Kaczynski (2016, 2018) – should be clearly distinguished from that of authors such as Marx, who thought that modernity and innovation were good but would only be sustainable and bring general benefit under a different economic system than capitalism. The position of the radical critics is that sustained innovation is in some sense impious because it disrupts a natural order and creates a way of living that runs against our nature as living creatures. The conclusion is that it will have catastrophic ecological and social consequences unless it is arrested and then reversed.

The response to this kind of argument is straightforward: it is empirically false. As Ridley argues and authors such as Julian Simon have shown, the effect of technological innovation has been and continues to be to reduce the impact of human beings on the environment. The pattern is for an older way of doing things to be enhanced by innovation and pushed to a limit and scale where it does indeed start to have an adverse impact. At that point, however, the tinkering and exchange-based process that Ridley describes leads to further innovation that resolves the problem. A current example is farming, particularly livestock farming, which is having a negative impact on the biosphere but looks set to be replaced almost entirely, due to innovations such as the development of cultured meat. As far as human well-being is concerned, the obvious rejoinder is that in most cases technophobes and neo-luddites do not show any enthusiasm for abandoning the results of innovation in their own life (with some honourable exceptions). The overwhelming majority of people everywhere would choose innovation and its results over the life of their ancestors.

Are innovation and growth sustainable?

A different argument is that innovation has brought great benefits but that it and the world we live in are unsustainable and will not continue. The usual case here is that innovation and growth cannot continue indefinitely because of the physical limits of the world. While true in extremis, most of the arguments in this vein are again refuted by the facts. Moreover, as the lecture points out, the key resource for innovation is knowledge and ideas and the way these are combined and recombined as a result of human interaction. This is so large as to be near infinite as far as we are concerned. The more serious argument relates to one resource in particular, energy, or more precisely usable energy and above all fossil fuels.

The thesis here is that the growth we have seen in the modern world is not the result of innovation but rather because of humanity having made use of the accumulated energy in fossil fuels. In this view, to the extent that we have higher levels of innovation now, this is a consequence of economic growth rather than a cause. (The further argument is that there was extensive innovation in the past without this leading to growth – the missing ingredient was energy.) The problem with this view is not that we will ever physically run out of fossil fuels or energy. Rather the challenge is that with time it takes ever increasing amounts of energy to get oil in particular out of the ground. This is measured by the EROEI (energy returned on energy invested) ratio. In the early part of the twentieth century it took the energy equivalent of one barrel of oil to get nearly a hundred actual barrels of oil out of the ground, but that ratio is now around one to twenty and declining. The common argument that we can simply replace fossil fuels with other, renewable, energy sources is rejected on two grounds. Firstly, the EROEI of renewables is too low to support a complex industrial civilisation (once the energy costs of producing things such as wind turbines and solar panels are taken into account) and there are theoretical reasons why this will not change. Secondly, there are things that can be done with petroleum in particular that cannot be done with any renewable energy because the latter is too diffuse and hard to store – oil by contrast contains a large amount of usable energy in a very light and compact form.

If this is true then modern growth will slowly come to an end, regardless of how much innovation there is, and we will revert to the historical norm (over a period of about seventy to two hundred years – most of the authors who take this view think that the process has already begun) (Greer 2017, 2019). As growth declines, and with it trade and exchange, so will innovation, which will also return to the historically normal pattern. This argument deserves to be taken seriously and its critique of renewable energy is pointed and effective, given current technology. The point, however, is that we can actually see what kind of innovation it is that we need to resolve this challenge: a means of storing, transporting and most of all compressing usable energy, from whatever source (a super battery if you will). If the model of innovation as a process presented by Matt Ridley is correct, then unless something else changes we should expect to see innovations that will do this happen in the way that he describes, by many piecemeal changes brought about by the interaction of large numbers of people (as he says, we are already seeing significant development in battery technology). Of course, it is possible that this will not happen, perhaps because the necessary innovations and discoveries will not happen in time. In that case our future is indeed bleak. However, the chances are that the innovation will happen – so long as other factors do not change in ways that hamper the innovative process.

Has innovation slowed down?

A different argument that has been made by a number of economists and others is that innovation actually peaked some time ago and that there are structural reasons for this. This argument was made by Jonathan Huebner in 2005 and has been elaborated by others, notably Tyler Cowen, Theodore Modis and Robert J. Gordon (Huebner 2005; Cowen 2011; Modis 2002; Gordon 2000). The argument here is that the pace of innovation as measured by a number of indices has slowed down significantly in the last thirty to forty years. This is held to explain the definite decline in growth rates in developed economies since the 1970s. According to this view the peak of innovation or at least of innovations that led to significant changes in productivity took place in the later nineteenth and early twentieth century. Since then, the argument goes, we have been basically filling in the gaps and refining those earlier fundamental breakthroughs. Much of this work, particularly by Modis, is aimed at the arguments of authors such as Hans Moravec (1990) and Ray Kurzweil (2006) that we are actually seeing accelerating innovation, which will lead us to a technological singularity in the near future (as mentioned earlier). The argument of the sceptics is that innovation, like most processes, is self-limiting and typically follows an S-shaped curve. Initially there is an accelerating rate of invention and innovation but the pace of innovation gradually slows and eventually flattens out. The commonest explanation for this cites one of the phenomena that Matt Ridley discusses in his lecture. Innovation leads to increased specialisation (as time is freed up so that, for example, we no longer need to have 80 per cent of the working population tied up in farming) and an increasingly elaborate division of labour. In other words, it leads to a higher level of social complexity. The problem in this view is that this greater complexity eventually makes effective innovation more difficult because it raises the cost of making the crucial personal and intellectual connections. In that case innovation is indeed an ultimately self-limiting process or at least one that has lengthy pauses.

The question of whether or not innovation has actually slowed down is actually a difficult one to resolve, because much of the debate is qualitative rather than purely quantitative. The argument is not simply that there are fewer patents, but rather that the innovations we are now getting are relatively trivial and not life transforming or productivity enhancing in the way that earlier ones such as electricity and the internal combustion engine were. There are two responses to this. This first is that it is simply too soon to tell if many of the more recent innovations will have as big an effect as those earlier ones or not. One of the main points that Matt Ridley makes in his lecture is precisely relevant here: we tend to systematically overestimate the impact of innovation in the short run and underestimate its long-run impact. This kind of argument gets support in the work of David Edgerton (2019), particularly his book *The Shock of the Old*. At first sight this looks like the antithesis to the case made by Ridley, as he argues that in histories of technology novelty is exaggerated while we overlook the persistence and staying power of older established techniques and technologies and even the revival in some cases of previously abandoned technologies. As he says, popular magazines are full of technologies and innovations that were meant to happen and transform the world but did not, while very old technologies continue without people noticing. The picture he paints, however, is very much in line with that of Ridley. Innovation is not a matter of heroic inventors or major transformative breakthroughs as much as a process of piecemeal changes brought about by tinkering and trial and error by individuals – the role of large-scale research and development is overestimated – and it is the cumulative effect of all of these individually minor changes and marginal improvements that is transformative. Most innovations fail, often because while technically feasible they are economically too costly or because they try to combine incompatible functions (supersonic passenger transport is an example of the former, flying cars of the latter). This means that the process of innovation is both fast and slow in the modern world: fast because ideas and experiments take place in ever larger numbers and at a higher frequency; slow because it takes time for the small changes to add up to something radical.

The other response to the alleged slowing down of innovation is that this is real but is not due to an endogenous factor such as the feedback effects of the greater complexity produced by innovation. Rather it is because of political and social changes. This argument has great force and relates directly to one of the main points of Ridley's lecture and perhaps the greatest threat facing the innovative process of modernity today.

Major threats to innovation and growth

Given what Ridley argues about the social basis of innovation and so ultimately of intensive growth and the modern world, then ideas and beliefs or public policies or laws that hinder that process or even stop it can have the (probably unintended) result of stopping innovation. If, as I argue, the sustained innovation of modernity was not the inevitable result of certain factors reaching a critical level but only happened because other structural forces that had previously prevented that kind of take-off were overcome, then it is perfectly possible that either deliberately or inadvertently we will bring about a return to the historical norm. The last two and a half centuries of sustained innovation and growth will indeed be just another episode of a much longer history.

There are three kinds of dynamic that might do this. The first is the effect of laws and institutions that are in theory designed to encourage innovation but which, given the understanding of it presented here, will actually choke it off. The main example of this, which Ridley cites, is intellectual property (IP). In theory patents and copyright are supposed to encourage risky innovation by granting the inventor a time-limited monopoly which will yield a monopoly rent (super normal income). There are many problems with this, to put it mildly. Quite apart from the philosophical problem that property rights are a response to the scarcity of resources and the conflicts this gives rise to, whereas information is an abundant non-scarce resource, there are practical difficulties. The major empirical problem is that there is no clear evidence that historically patents have encouraged productive innovation. The theory presented by Ridley leads in fact to the opposite conclusion, that they hamper innovation. If innovation is the product of the exchange of ideas and the efforts of enterprising individuals to improve or adapt things that others have done before them, then anything that makes this process more costly or drawn out, or in extremis prevents it entirely, will block innovation. In terms of the present, the evidence is strong that the kind of intellectual property regime advocated and enforced by the US in particular hampers innovation through the copying and improvement of existing technology. It also provides ample opportunities for rent seeking in the shape of patent trolls who use patents simply as a means to raise income through vexatious lawsuits, and creates a class of IP rentiers who gain wealth and income not by innovation but through the monopoly they have been granted by the state. In addition, IP increasingly undermines real property rights in actual physical commodities by limiting the use their owners can make of them in all kinds of intrusive ways – this also hinders innovation.

The second problem is that of attitudes, ideas and beliefs and the politics they give rise to in modern democracies. The challenge here is the persistence of fear and unease about innovation and the change it brings, which leads to pressure from two sources for measures that will slow down or stop particular innovations or even the innovation in general. The first comes from people who have indeed lost out from the effects of particular innovations or who believe that they have lost even when that is not true. The second is from people who have gained from previous innovations or the existing state of affairs and fear that continuing innovations will undermine their position. Together these two kinds of pressure, one from threatened elites, the other from a wider popular movement, can produce a very powerful politics that deliberately tries to slow down change or to prevent it entirely. We can see this for example in resistance to 'sharing economy' applications such as Uber. Much contemporary politics, such as resistance to migration or support for protectionism, ultimately reflects a fear of innovation and change and a focus upon costs and losers from change rather than benefits and gainers. In addition, there are a number of ideas that have become very influential and which reflect this outlook. One of the most powerful, which Ridley discusses, is that of the precautionary principle, the idea that we should not have innovation until we are sure that an innovation will not have harmful effects. Since we can never be certain of that, this is in practice and if taken seriously a call for no change or innovation of any kind. In addition, because in many cases not doing anything or not innovating is itself risky, the argument is incoherent and does not provide a real guide to action. To the extent that it influences political debate, however, it can have very harmful effects. (The contrary view is the 'proactionary principle' that we should try to identify problems and challenges as early as possible so that the innovative process can produce solutions to them sooner.)

However, the biggest problem is the third one. Bad institutions such as intellectual property and politics motivated by a misguided fear of innovation can do harm, but they cannot now stop the innovative process unless they operate on a worldwide scale. If they do not, the process will continue in those parts of the world less affected by them. So, although there may be parts of the planet that stagnate the world as a whole will not. In addition, the parts of the world that do go down the route of arresting innovation will fall behind those that do not, by a number of measures, and eventually this will become insupportable. However, there is a development that threatens to create a global check to innovation. This is the growth of supranational regulatory regimes such as the EU, and the global network of harmonised regulations created by so-called trade deals. Although such deals are intended to promote trade and exchange by removing what are called non-tariff barriers to trade (essentially, conflicting regulatory regimes that prevent products being freely traded across regulatory borders), they do so by harmonising regulatory regimes. This creates an increasingly global and standardised pattern of regulation.

This is very dangerous for the innovative process because it threatens to revive the incentives facing rulers that were described earlier, but this time on a global scale. One of the main reasons why some ruling classes eventually supported innovation instead of trying to check it was the reality that they faced of being in competition with other elites that controlled other parts of the planet's surface. They could only enforce regulations in the geographical areas that they controlled and to do so at a high level disadvantaged them in the competition. In addition, for the greater part of modern history (up until the 1930s or even the 1950s) regulation was fairly light and general in content rather than specific and detailed. Now it is huge in scope, enormous in volume, and amazingly detailed and precise. What this does in a whole range of areas (pharmaceuticals being only the most glaring example) is to restrict the innovative process and create barriers to the kinds of trade and exchange that drive it.

However, trying to resolve this by removing the clash of regulations and with it the competition between regulatory regimes is to fall into what we may call the trap of empire. Empires that unite a large part of the world create an extensive area of stable government and exchange. Initially this creates more exchange and economic dynamism. However, the incentives for the rulers of the empire to control and check innovation are extremely powerful and they no longer need to fear competition from other elites in the way that rulers of smaller states do. The current trend is to create something like a global regulatory order, a kind of world empire in fact. This would surely stop innovation in its tracks and restore the incentives and conditions that led popular processes and elite action to check innovation for most of recorded history.

Matt Ridley explains clearly what innovation is, what it derives from, and the benefits it has brought. He also sets out some of the dangers we now face, both political and cultural, and institutional. However, I fear he is still too optimistic. To think that the modern world of innovation is natural or inevitable is to fail to realise how contingent it is and how much its appearance was the outcome of chance events. We should not take it for granted and we should be always aware of the constant danger that often well-meaning moves, along with the influence of mistaken ideas and sentiments, will bring it to a halt and restore the world of our ancestors.

References

Cowen, T. (2004) *Creative Destruction: How Globalization Is Changing the World's Cultures.* Princeton University Press.

Cowen, T. (2011) *The Great Stagnation: How America Ate All of the Low Hanging Fruit of Modern History, Got Sick, and Will (Eventually) Feel Better.* New York: Penguin.

Davies, S. J. (2019) *The Wealth Explosion: The Nature and Origins of Modernity.* Brighton: Edward Everett Root.

Edgerton, D. (2019) *The Shock of the Old: Technology and Global History Since 1900.* London: Profile.

Edwards, R. A. (2013) Redefining industrial revolution: Song China and England (https://economicdynamics.org/meetpa pers/2013/paper_351.pdf).

Goldstone, J. A. (2002) Efflorescences and economic growth in world history: rethinking the 'rise of the West' and the Industrial Revolution. *Journal of World History* 13(2): 323–89.

Gordon, R. J. (2000) Does the 'new economy' measure up to the great inventions of the past? *Journal of Economic Perspectives* 14(4): 49–74.

Greer, J. M. (2017) *The Retro Future: Looking to the Past to Reinvent the Future.* Gabriola Island, BC: New Society Publishers.

Greer, J. M. (2019) *The Long Descent: A User's Guide to the End of the Industrial Age.* Danville, IL: Founders House Publishing.

Huebner, J. (2005) A possible declining trend for worldwide innovation. *Technological Forecasting and Social Change* 72(8): 980–86.

Kaczynski, T. J. (2016) *Anti-Tech Revolution: Why and How.* Scottsdale, AZ: Fitch and Madison.

Kaczynski, T. J. (2018) [1995] *Industrial Society and Its Future.* Pub House Books.

Kealey, T. (1996) *The Economic Laws of Scientific Research.* London: Palgrave Macmillan.

Kurzweil, R. (2006) *The Singularity Is Near.* London: Duckworth.

McCloskey, D. (2007) *The Bourgeois Virtues: Ethics for an Age of Commerce.* Chicago University Press.

McCloskey, D. (2010) *Bourgeois Dignity: Why Economics Can't Explain the Modern World.* Chicago University Press.

McCloskey, D. (2017) *Bourgeois Equality: How Ideas, Not Capital or Institutions Enriched the World.* Chicago University Press.

Modis, T. (2002) The limits of complexity and change. *The Futurist* May–June, pp. 26–32.

Mokyr, J. (2011) *The Enlightened Economy: Britain and the Industrial Revolution, 1700–1850.* London: Penguin.

Mokyr, J. (2018) *A Culture of Growth: The Origins of the Modern Economy.* Princeton University Press.

Moravec, H. (1990) *Mind Children: The Future of Robot and Human Intelligence.* Harvard University Press.

Rustow, D. A. (1980) *Freedom and Power: A Historical Critique of Civilisation.* Princeton University Press.

Scott, J. C. (1976)*The Moral Economy of the Peasant: Rebellion and Subsistence in Southeast Asia.* Princeton University Press.

Thompson, E. P. (1991) *Customs in Common.* New York: New Press.

Ward-Perkins, B. (2006) *The Fall of Rome and the End of Civilisation.* Oxford University Press.

ABOUT THE IEA

The Institute is a research and educational charity (No. CC 235 351), limited by guarantee. Its mission is to improve understanding of the fundamental institutions of a free society by analysing and expounding the role of markets in solving economic and social problems.

The IEA achieves its mission by:

- a high-quality publishing programme
- conferences, seminars, lectures and other events
- outreach to school and college students
- brokering media introductions and appearances

The IEA, which was established in 1955 by the late Sir Antony Fisher, is an educational charity, not a political organisation. It is independent of any political party or group and does not carry on activities intended to affect support for any political party or candidate in any election or referendum, or at any other time. It is financed by sales of publications, conference fees and voluntary donations.

In addition to its main series of publications, the IEA also publishes (jointly with the University of Buckingham), *Economic Affairs*.

The IEA is aided in its work by a distinguished international Academic Advisory Council and an eminent panel of Honorary Fellows. Together with other academics, they review prospective IEA publications, their comments being passed on anonymously to authors. All IEA papers are therefore subject to the same rigorous independent refereeing process as used by leading academic journals.

IEA publications enjoy widespread classroom use and course adoptions in schools and universities. They are also sold throughout the world and often translated/reprinted.

Since 1974 the IEA has helped to create a worldwide network of 100 similar institutions in over 70 countries. They are all independent but share the IEA's mission.

Views expressed in the IEA's publications are those of the authors, not those of the Institute (which has no corporate view), its Managing Trustees, Academic Advisory Council members or senior staff.

Members of the Institute's Academic Advisory Council, Honorary Fellows, Trustees and Staff are listed on the following page.

The Institute gratefully acknowledges financial support for its publications programme and other work from a generous benefaction by the late Professor Ronald Coase.

Killjoys: A Critique of Paternalism
Christopher Snowdon
ISBN 978-0-255-36749-3; £12.50

Financial Stability without Central Banks
George Selgin, Kevin Dowd and Mathieu Bédard
ISBN 978-0-255-36752-3; £10.00

Against the Grain: Insights from an Economic Contrarian
Paul Ormerod
ISBN 978-0-255-36755-4; £15.00

Ayn Rand: An Introduction
Eamonn Butler
ISBN 978-0-255-36764-6; £12.50

Capitalism: An Introduction
Eamonn Butler
ISBN 978-0-255-36758-5; £12.50

Opting Out: Conscience and Cooperation in a Pluralistic Society
David S. Oderberg
ISBN 978-0-255-36761-5; £12.50

Getting the Measure of Money: A Critical Assessment of UK Monetary Indicators
Anthony J. Evans
ISBN 978-0-255-36767-7; £12.50

Socialism: The Failed Idea That Never Dies
Kristian Niemietz
ISBN 978-0-255-36770-7; £17.50

Top Dogs and Fat Cats: The Debate on High Pay
Edited by J. R. Shackleton
ISBN 978-0-255-36773-8; £15.00

School Choice around the World … And the Lessons We Can Learn
Edited by Pauline Dixon and Steve Humble
ISBN 978-0-255-36779-0; £15.00

School of Thought: 101 Great Liberal Thinkers
Eamonn Butler
ISBN 978-0-255-36776-9; £12.50

Raising the Roof: How to Solve the United Kingdom's Housing Crisis
Edited by Jacob Rees-Mogg and Radomir Tylecote
ISBN 978-0-255-36782-0; £12.50

Other IEA publications

Comprehensive information on other publications and the wider work of the IEA can be found at www.iea.org.uk. To order any publication please see below.

Personal customers

Orders from personal customers should be directed to the IEA:

Clare Rusbridge
IEA
2 Lord North Street
FREEPOST LON10168
London SW1P 3YZ
Tel: 020 7799 8911, Fax: 020 7799 2137
Email: sales@iea.org.uk

Trade customers

All orders from the book trade should be directed to the IEA's distributor:

NBN International (IEA Orders)
Orders Dept.
NBN International
10 Thornbury Road
Plymouth PL6 7PP
Tel: 01752 202301, Fax: 01752 202333
Email: orders@nbninternational.com

IEA subscriptions

The IEA also offers a subscription service to its publications. For a single annual payment (currently £42.00 in the UK), subscribers receive every monograph the IEA publishes. For more information please contact:

Clare Rusbridge
Subscriptions
IEA
2 Lord North Street
FREEPOST LON10168
London SW1P 3YZ
Tel: 020 7799 8911, Fax: 020 7799 2137
Email: crusbridge@iea.org.uk